A Short Collection of Proverbs from India

A Short Collection of Proverbs from India

Compiled by:

Sanjay Saxena

To order additional copies of this book, contact:
Xlibris Corporation
1-888-795-4274
www.Xlibris.com
Orders@Xlibris.com
49393

Dedicated to

Guru Omkar Prasad

My parents Indira and Eshwar Raj

My lifelines Madhu, Kunal, Anoushka:
Without you this would not have happened

Didi, Jeejaji, Uday, Neeraj and Adarsh Bhai

"First day a guest, second day a pest."

"When the cat gets weak, the rat asks her out for a date."

"Don't make holes in the plate that you eat from."

"In a forest it is the straight trees that get cut first."

"One who is too sweet will be crushed, just like sugarcane."

"In its own territory even a dog behaves like a tiger."

"In order to pluck the fruit, you have to climb the tree."

"A good horseman is one who has taken a fall many a time."

"When you blow dust, a lot of it comes into your eyes."

"People who live in glass homes, should not throw stones at others' homes."

"Do not challenge a crocodile inside water."

"One who has been burnt with hot milk is careful even while drinking milk shake."

"The mighty trees might get uprooted in a storm but the little grass survives."

"A nail cutter cannot be used to cut a tree."

"You cannot straighten a dog's tail."

"There are three kinds of persons in this world:
   a) Those who talk and do not act
   b) Those who act and do not talk
   c) Those who talk and also act."

"He who cannot dance blames the dance floor."

"Do not stretch your legs beyond the length of the bed sheet."

"When you point a finger at others, remember the other three are pointing at you."

"Clouds that roar seldom pour."

"An elephant has two sets of teeth; it shows off with one and eats with the other."

"A half full pot shakes a lot."

"Amongst the blind, the one-eyed is the king."

"One stroke of the iron smith is equal to hundred strokes of a gold smith."

"Do good and forget about it."

"Fruits don't ripen in a day."

"You cannot clap by just one hand."

"Sweet are the fruits of patience."

"A lotus flower grows uninfluenced by
its not so clean surroundings."

"Turn your umbrella in the direction of rain."

"A bad diet is the mother of bad health."

"A sleeping man cannot awaken another sleeping man."

"Roses and thorns grow on the same stem."

"One and one makes eleven."

"When two Valentines agree, the priest has no say."

"Moonlight comes in the way of thief."

"Spoon can never taste curry."

"What needs to be done tomorrow, do it today;
what needs to be done today, do it now."

"The more honey you use, the sweeter the recipe becomes."

"When you are riding an elephant you don't have to be
afraid of dogs."

"Thousand razors cannot cut a tree."

"If the horse makes friends with grass, what will it eat?"

"An enemy's enemy is a friend."

"He who questions will not lose the path."

"From a distance even noise sounds like music."

"Even if you drink water sitting underneath a palm tree, people will think you are drinking toddy or palm wine."

"Action gives rise to good luck."

"Cream always comes to the top."

"Truth eventually will win."

"United we stand; divided we fall."

"Words spoken once cannot be taken back."

"He who aims at sky shoots higher than the one who aims at tree."

"A donkey does not know the value of saffron."

"Even walls have ears."

"Interest amount is more interesting than
the principal amount."

"Knowledge grows when it is shared and shrinks when it is not."

www.ingramcontent.com/pod-product-compliance
Lightning Source LLC
Chambersburg PA
CBHW031327290526
45784CB00014B/2402